A Brief History of the Smallwood Store *in Chokoloskee, Florida*

Marya Repko

ECITY • PUBLISHING

A Brief History of the Smallwood Store in Chokoloskee, FL

© 2015 text by Marya Repko
All rights reserved.

cover sketch of Smallwood Store courtesy of Matthew Goldman ("Constant Waterman")
Historic photographs in this book are from the Florida State Archives unless otherwise noted.

set in Century Schoolbook, 12/16pt
printed & bound in the USA
First Edition, Fourth Printing, May 2018

ABOUT THE TYPE FACE
The Century family of type was designed for Century Publishing in 1894 by typographer Linn Boyd Benton of American Type Founders and revised by his son Morris Fuller Benton. "Century Schoolbook" was commissioned in 1919 by textbook publisher Ginn & Co. and is known for its legibility.

ISBN 978-0-9830425-3-2

ECITY • PUBLISHING

P O Box 5033
Everglades City, FL, 34139
telephone (239) 695-2905
www.ecity-publishing.com

Other books from this publisher:
   A Brief History of the Everglades City Area
   The Story of Everglades City; A History for Younger Readers
   Historia de Everglades City (Spanish translation by Gloria Gutiérrez)
   A Brief History of the Fakahatchee
   A Brief History of Sanibel Island
   The Story of Sanibel Island; A History for Younger Readers
   Angel of the Swamp; Deaconess Harriet Bedell in the Everglades
   Grandma of the Glades; A Brief Biography of Marjory Stoneman Douglas
   Memories from Hadlyme; A Personal History of the East Haddam, CT, Area
   Women in the Everglades; Pioneers and Early Environmentalists
   The Story of Barron Collier; A History for Younger Readers

A Brief History of the Smallwood Store

PREFACE

As I was helping to organize the Smallwood Music Festival on January 31, 2015, I realized that a "Brief History" of the Store would be interesting reading for well-wishers in the audience and for visitors to the Store & Museum in future.

My thanks to Lynn Smallwood McMillin, founder of Ted Smallwood Store, Inc., a 501(c)(3) not-for-profit which operates the Store, for recollections about her grandparents Ted & Mamie and to other members of this historic family.

As always, my thanks to the diligent proof readers who responded to my call for help under time pressure. Any remaining mistakes are mine and I appreciate hearing from readers with suggestions or additions.

Marya Repko
Everglades City, FL
mrepko@earthlink.net
January, 2015

POSTSCRIPT
The successful White Pelican Festival was held in January 2017. See www.smallwoodstore.com for future events.

A Brief History of the Smallwood Store

A Brief History of the Smallwood Store

CONTENTS

BACKGROUND HISTORY 1

BEGINNINGS 5

TRADING POST 9

MOVING ON 11

NEXT GENERATION 13

MAKING A MUSEUM 15

CURRENT TIMES & TROUBLES 17

FURTHER READING 19

TIME LINE 22

A Brief History of the Smallwood Store

Florida in 1859. The Chokoloskee area was in Monroe County whose seat was Key West. In 1887 Lee County was established and in 1923 Collier County was formed. The newer counties included Chokoloskee.

A Brief History of the Smallwood Store

BACKGROUND HISTORY

When Ponce de Leon explored the west coast of Florida in 1521, he found villages of natives called Calusa. They were tall people, highly organized, and lived mainly from the bounty of the sea. They built large mounds from shells to keep them above flood level and dug canals as canoe routes.

The Spanish claimed Florida and tried to establish some settlements until the territory was exchanged with the British for Havana in 1763. Many of the Calusa had died from European diseases, to which they had no immunity, but what remained of them retreated to Cuba with the Spanish. Another treaty in 1783 gave Florida back to the Spanish who handed it over to the United States in 1821.

The American government was trying to move natives west of Mississippi so that white farmers could settle in the Carolinas and Georgia. Rather than be displaced to such a different environment, some of the tribes migrated south into Florida where they got into skirmishes with the pioneers already there. The settlers were defended by the U.S. Army.

The Seminole Wars continued for over 30 years until the only natives left had established themselves deep in the Everglades. Evidence of these wars is seen in the names around south Florida such as Fort

A Brief History of the Smallwood Store

Myers, Fort Lauderdale, Fort Pierce, plus others that have since fallen out of use (e.g., Fort Dallas is now Miami) or did not develop into cities.

When the Civil War began in 1861, Northerners who found themselves below the Mason-Dixon line headed to Key West, a Unionist stronghold. The island city was also a prosperous shipping port and the seat of Monroe County which stretched all along the southwest coast of Florida up to Fort Myers.

After hostilities ceased, many of these displaced Yankees drifted from the Keys onto mainland Florida; the Weeks brothers setting up farms in Everglades and Naples is an example. Soldiers who had been stationed in Florida returned to avail themselves of the pleasant climate. Farmers found the cold conditions in central Florida were unsuitable for growing marketable crops so moved south to find more suitable conditions.

There were no roads in southern Florida at that time. Transportation was by boat only so settlers sailed to the coastal islands such as Marco, Fakahatchee, and Chokoloskee or up the mouths of rivers. For example, the shell mound on Turner River was settled in 1874 by Captain R. B. Turner who had discovered it when he led an Army party to fight Seminoles near there in 1857.

A Brief History of the Smallwood Store

By 1887, there were enough people around the Fort Myers area to warrant a change in political boundaries and Lee County was carved out of Monroe. However, pioneers on the southern fringes still felt remote from civilization and continued to be mainly self-sufficient, growing or hunting or catching most of their food, and taking the law into their own hands.

In 1923 Barron Gift Collier, a large land owner in southwest Florida, agreed to complete the Tamiami Trail (from Tampa to Miami) across the Everglades if a new county were established with his name. The little farming village of Everglades was developed into the county seat and engineering headquarters for the road works. Chokoloskee, which Collier did not own, was included in his county.

The Trail was completed in 1928, changing the focus of transportation from water to land.

A Brief History of the Smallwood Store

Ted & Mamie Smallwood, owners of Smallwood's Store, settled on Chokoloskee Island in 1897 - Ted came to the 10,000 Islands in 1891, the year the post office was estab. on Chokoloskee. Mamie arrived early in 1896.

A Brief History of the Smallwood Store

BEGINNINGS

Charles Sherod ("Ted") Smallwood was born in 1873 in Mikesville, Columbia County, Florida. His mother died soon after he was born so he lived with his grandparents in Georgia for a few years and then with an aunt & uncle back in Mikesville. In 1883, they moved south to the Fort Ogden area near where his father Robert B. Smallwood had an orange grove.

In 1891 Ted sailed with his friend John Yeomans to Fakahatchee Island and Halfway Creek. He cut buttonwood to sell in Key West where it was used as charcoal for cooking. He recalled sailing in 1893 with vegetables and wood to the island city and bringing back the ballot boxes for the first election held in these parts.

As a young unencumbered wanderer, he went to the Miami area where he cleared land and did whatever work was required. He was familiar with the Peacock store in Coconut Grove, the Brickell trading post on the Miami River, and Julia Tuttle, the "Mother of Miami", who persuaded Henry Flagler to extend his Florida East Coast railway to the little village there in 1896.

Ted ventured further to Bimini with Yeomans where he "fooled around"[1] and took a quick visit to Nassau.

---

[1] Tebeau, *The Story of Chokoloskee Bay Country*, p.72

A Brief History of the Smallwood Store

Next, he went to Anna Maria Key on the west coast of Florida in 1894 to cut buttonwood that he sold in Ybor City, the section of Tampa where Cubans rolled cigars.

Finally, in 1896, Ted came back to the Ten Thousand Islands with Isaac Yeomans and ran a mail boat from Chokoloskee to Everglade to Marco Island for $1 per day, three times a week. He said, "That was the worst job I ever had."[2] On the return trip he would stop at Panther Key to deliver supplies to the old pirate Juan Gomez, thought to be well over 100 years old when he died in an accident in 1905.

Ted then worked for Daniel David House on the Turner River as a farm laborer and met young Mamie, D.D.'s daughter, and fell in love. They married in 1897 and moved to Chokoloskee two years later.

By that time, the island had been settled by the Santini family who left their native Corsica fearing prosecution after helping Napoleon to escape. Among the produce they grew for sale were avocadoes. Some trees from the original stock are still bearing fruit; "pears" or "alligator pears" in the native lingo does not mean the sweet fruit we associate with apples.

---

[2] Tebeau, *The Story of Chokoloskee Bay Country*, p.75

A Brief History of the Smallwood Store

In 1899, Ted bought the Santini property near a Calusa shell mound on the south side of Chokoloskee and then opened a store in his house when he was appointed Postmaster in 1906. The old "sage of Chokoloskee", C.G. McKinney, had been granted a Post Office in 1892 on condition that sailboats could collect mail three times a week from Key West.

Ted's store was the scene of the famous *Killing of Mister Watson* in 1910, memorialized in fiction by Peter Matthiessen in his trilogy of books (see list on page 20). Coincidentally, a previous book about the same incident by the husband and wife team of A. B. and Barbara Matthiessen was published in 1955 with the title *The Singing and the Gold*. There seems to be no connection between the authors.

As for Ted, he commented about Watson:[3]
> He used to trade with me for years. I never had any trouble with him.

And, as for the killing in front of his Store, he said:[4]
> I did not want any part of it. Watson had done nothing to me ... We heard guns going off and I heard Mrs. Watson say, 'My God, they have killed Mr. Watson.' ... A good while after I went to the landing and Mr. Watson was lying there dead.

---

[3] Tebeau, *The Story of Chokoloskee Bay Country,* p.79
[4] Tebeau, *The Story of Chokoloskee Bay Country,* p.81

A Brief History of the Smallwood Store

A Brief History of the Smallwood Store

TRADING POST

As Smallwood children came along, it was decided in 1917 to build a proper store on the waterfront near the family home. Included was the little room with mail boxes to house the Post Office which can still be seen today just to the right of the front entrance.

In the bay, Ted dredged a channel to build stilt houses where commercial fishermen could offload their catch which was then taken by run boats to market in Key West or Fort Myers or Punta Gorda.

He also found fresh water and dug a well. Before that, water was collected in cisterns over the rainy summer to be used during the dry winter season. The new Store was raised on stilts in 1924 just in time to avoid disaster in the 1926 hurricane.

Locals remember walking down Mamie Street (named after Ted's wife) to collect their letters and buy stamps for sending correspondence. They also shopped at the Store for hardware and household staples (e.g., flour, sugar, coffee). What was not in stock was ordered from the Sears Roebuck catalogs.

Seminoles came, too. They carried animal skins and deer meat in their canoes to sell to Ted at the Trading Post. With the profits, they bought calico for their bright patchwork clothing and grits to make sofkee (a corn mash).

Ted learned their language and was considered a friend because he treated them fairly. They would often camp near the Store for several days before paddling back to villages in the Glades hinterland. The Seminoles trusted Ted enough to let him give them white man's medicines when they got sick with non-native diseases like influenza.

Ted's daughter Thelma remembered that if her father was not in the Store, "They would point to what they wanted and pay for it an item at a time, Indian fashion."[5]

After the Tamiami Trail across the Everglades was completed by Barron Collier in 1928, the Indians traded less at the Store and concentrated on tourism.

---

[5] Tebeau, *The Story of Chokoloskee Bay Country,* p.58

MOVING ON

Ted handed over the Post Office and Store to his daughter Thelma in 1941. Mamie died in 1943 and Ted passed away in 1951.

"Mamie's Road", begun in 1935 to Chokoloskee from the mainland, never got across the water. When the Army Corps of Engineers finally tackled the project, they suggested a new route which was completed in 1956. The original road became Plantation Parkway leading to a settlement on Halfway Creek.

Until the causeway was completed, youngsters went by school boat to Everglades. On Saturday nights they rowed there to attend the movies in the "big city" where they enjoyed the rare treat of ice cream and the sight of the electric street lights.[6]

---

[6] author interviews, *in passim*

A Brief History of the Smallwood Store

Hollywood came to Chokoloskee during the winter of 1957-58 to film sequences in "Wind Across the Everglades", the story of plume hunters in the Glades. The gang, led by rotund Burl Ives, is pursued by game warden Christopher Plummer. The action starts in Miami but was shot in a transformed Everglades City with Gypsy Rose Lee as a "madame" in a saloon trying to entice the hero.

The script was written by Budd Schulberg (author of "On the Waterfront") with technical advice from Bud Kirk of Marco Island. The movie was produced by Schulberg's brother Stuart whose son K.C. is planning another film set in the area.

A Brief History of the Smallwood Store

NEXT GENERATION

The causeway opened up Chokoloskee to tourism and the next generation of Smallwoods took advantage of new opportunities.

Nancy was the youngest of the Smallwood children, born in 1924. She married Alton Carlton (A.C.) Hancock, another local resident. He built boats in the yard near the Store *(left in photo below)*, including the school boat, and the "ACE" fishing boat which is currently being restored. A.C. was a Collier County Commissioner from 1960 to 1972.

The Hancocks built the Blue Heron Motel and Marina on Mamie Street which they operated from 1956 until 1999 when they retired and sold the property to the Seminole Tribe of Florida.

A.C. died in 2004 and Nancy passed away in 2006. They were both buried near Ted and Mamie in the private Smallwood cemetery on Chokoloskee. The oldest grave, dated 1916, is that of D.D. House.

A Brief History of the Smallwood Store

Robert (Bob) developed the nearby Parkway R.V. Village and Marina with its 8-room motel. When he died in 1985 it passed to his daughter Iris, a talented artist. It was sold in 1991.

Ted, Jr., and his wife Clara owned and operated a boat dock and trailer park in Everglades City. They sold it in the late 1980s. He was well-known as a sports fishing guide and Clara excelled at fly-fishing ties. A frequent visitor said, "You would never meet a more loving, giving couple as Clara & Ted ... We were treated as family."[7] Ted died in 1993 and Clara in 2012.

Subsequent offspring of the family are active in the area and the youngest can boast of being a sixth-generation Floridian.

---

[7] email to the author, 1/26/15

A Brief History of the Smallwood Store

MAKING A MUSEUM

Thelma served as Postmaster until she retired in 1973 at age 69. She died in 1982 and the Store closed after 65 years.

Ted and Mamie's granddaughter Lynn worried about the old building and all the history it contained. It had been added to the National Register of Historic Places (#74000612) in 1974.

Lynn and her friend Nancy Hollister began cleaning up the premises, registered a non-profit corporation (Ted Smallwood Store, Inc.), and looked for funding.

In 1989 the Store finally re-opened as the Museum we know today, watched over by a life-like manikin of Ted resting in his rocking chair. The gift shop features books about local history and patchwork clothing made by Seminoles.

A Brief History of the Smallwood Store

Relations with the native tribe were good. In 1991 they participated in the first Seminole Festival at the Store where the guest of honor was 101-year-old Marjory Stoneman Douglas, famous for her book *The Everglades: River of Grass*. A number of Seminole Festivals followed featuring folk music, crafts, and Indian food.

Several performances of "The Killing of Mister Watson" were given under the Museum starring former Collier County Commissioner Jim Coletta as the famous bad guy.

Marjory Stoneman Douglas with Chief James Billie at the first Seminole Festival at the Smallwood Store in 1991.
photo courtesy of the Seminole Tribe of Florida

A Brief History of the Smallwood Store

CURRENT TIMES & TROUBLES

The leadership of the Seminole Tribe changed in 2001 when the charismatic Chief James Billie was removed as chairman. In 2004, the new regime sold the Mamie Street property to Florida Georgia Grove, LLC, a development company from Sebring, FL.

FGG had plans to expand the marina but the road bisecting their property was thought to be an inconvenience. On April 14, 2011, they "chopped [it] to rubble during a surprise bulldozer terrorism ambush in the early dawn hours."[8] and erected a fence blocking access to the Store (and to some of the residents of Parkway R.V. Village).

It was not until September 15 of that year that the Collier County Circuit Court ordered FGG to take down the fence and to restore the road within 30 days. However, the road was a bumpy dirt path until another court case forced FGG to pave it at the end of March 2012.

There was further unpleasantness on April 24, 2014, when FGG bulldozed some of what appears to be a shell mound left by the ancient Calusa Indians.

---

[8] "Showdown at the Collier County Courthouse" by Peter B. Gallagher, *The Seminole Tribune*, 9/27/11.

A Brief History of the Smallwood Store

The area is rich in ancient history as well as more recent pioneering lore. According to Czech-American anthropologist Aleš Hrdlička writing in 1922;[9]

> Chokaloskee Island ... appears to have been one of the most important centers of Indian settlements on the southwestern coast of the peninsula ... The place should, by all means, be mapped out by a competent archeologist or surveyor before buildings and the removal of shells for various purposes will obliterate its original aspect still further. It must have been quite a metropolis of Indians.

Unfortunately, the preservation of our heritage is often ignored.

The 6 months when the road was closed and further 5½ months when it was almost impassable caused the Museum to languish with few or no visitors and, thus, suffer a dramatic fall in revenue while expenses for legal fees mounted.

Fundraisers, so far, have included a breakfast with author Carl Hiaasen in April 2012 and the Music Festival in January 2015 which inspired this book.

---

[9] Hrdlička, Aleš, *The Anthropology of Florida,* 1922: Florida State Historical Society, Deland, FL, p.35.

FURTHER READING

Ted Smallwood's reminiscences in Tebeau's book about Chokoloskee reveal an extraordinary memory for names and details and events that occurred many years previously when he was a youngster. His daughter Thelma continues in the main part of the book to describe life at the Store when the Seminoles came to trade.

Professor Tebeau wrote the little volume in celebration of the opening of the causeway but is better known as the author of the definitive history of Collier County.

Many of the photos in this current book come from the Florida State Archives whose website
   www.floridamemory.com
contains a wealth of historical images.

To learn more about the Smallwood Store, see
   www.smallwoodstore.com
where you can make a donation to the legal fund.

REFERENCE BOOKS

Brown, Loren G, *Totch: A Life in the Everglades,*
    1993: University Press of Florida, Gainesville, FL

Kersey, Harry A., Jr., *Pelts, Plumes, and Hides; White Traders among the Seminole Indians 1870-1930,*
    1975: University Presses of Florida, Gainesville, FL

McIvor, Stuart, *True Tales of the Everglades,*
    1990: Florida Flair Books, Miami, FL

Tebeau, Charlton W., *The Story of the Chokoloskee Bay Country; with Reminiscences of Pioneer C.S. "Ted" Smallwood,* 1996: Florida Flair Books, Miami, FL (original edition 1955, University of Miami Press)

Tebeau, Charlton W., *Florida's Last Frontier; The History of Collier County,* 1966: University of Miami Press, Miami

FICTION

Magers, Rick, *The Ghosts of Chokoloskee,*
    2014: Grizzly Bookz Publishing, Chokoloskee, FL

Matthiessen, A. B., *The Singing and the Gold; A Novel of a Hidden Drama in American Folk History,*
    1955: Doubleday, New York

Matthiessen, Peter, *Killing Mister Watson,*
    1990: Random House, New York

Matthiessen, Peter, *Lost Man's River,*
    1997: Random House, New York

Matthiessen, Peter, *Bone by Bone,*
    1999: Random House, New York

Matthiessen, Peter, *Shadow Country,*
    2008: Random House, New York

A Brief History of the Smallwood Store

The school boat behind the Store took older students to Everglades City before the causeway was completed.

Ernest Coe, father of Everglades National Park which opened in 1947, talking with Ted at the Smallwood Store.

A Brief History of the Smallwood Store

TIME LINE

1513 Ponce de Leon claimed Florida for the Spanish
1821 United States acquired Florida from the Spanish
1845 Florida established as a state
1850 Florida granted the "swamp and overflowed" lands
1857 end of Seminole Wars
1866 end of Civil War between the states
1873 **C.S. (Ted) Smallwood born**
1879 **Mamie Ulala House born**
1887 Lee County established
1891 **Ted Smallwood visited 10,000 Islands**
1896 **Ted Smallwood returned to 10,000 Islands**
1897 **Ted Smallwood and Mamie House married**
1899 **Ted & Mamie Smallwood moved to Chokoloskee**

1906 **Ted Smallwood appointed Postmaster**
1910 hurricane
1917 **Ted Smallwood built new Store**
1918 **Ted Smallwood dredged the channel**
1918 **Ted Smallwood dug a fresh-water well**
1923 Collier County established
1924 **Ted Smallwood raised the Store on stilts**
1926 hurricane
1928 Tamiami Trail completed

1941 **Thelma Smallwood became Postmaster**
1943 **Mamie Smallwood died**
1947 Everglades National Park opened
1951 **Ted Smallwood died**
1956 Chokoloskee causeway completed
1960 Hurricane Donna
1973 **Thelma Smallwood retired**
1982 **Thelma Smallwood died**
1982 **Store closed**
1989 **Museum opened**
1991 **First Seminole Festival at the Store**
1999 Blue Heron property sold to Seminole Tribe
2004 Blue Heron property sold to Florida Georgia Grove

www.ingramcontent.com/pod-product-compliance
Lightning Source LLC
Chambersburg PA
CBHW052031290426
44112CB00014B/2466